W9-BLH-545

ALEXANDER
GRAHAM BELL

ALEXANDER GRAHAM BELL

BY PATRICIA RYON QUIRI

FRANKLIN WATTS
NEW YORK LONDON TORONTO SYDNEY 1991
A FIRST BOOK

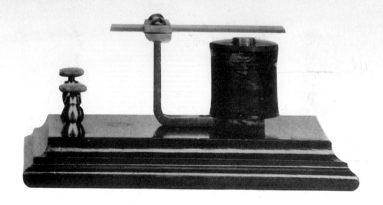

For my husband, Bob, with love

Photo credits for ALEXANDER GRAHAM BELL

Cover photographs courtesy of The New York Public Library Picture Collection

Photographs courtesy of: AT&T Archives: pp. 2, 3, 8, 20, 26, 35, 36, 41, 45, 52 (The Bell Family/National Geographic Society), 54 top; Alexander Graham Bell National Historical Park: pp. 13, 17, 29, 30, 38, 48, 55; Historical Picture Service, Chicago: pp. 15, 44, 50; The Bettmann Archive: pp. 24, 42, 43, 54 bottom.

Library of Congress Cataloging-in-Publication Data

Quiri, Patricia Ryon.
   Alexander Graham Bell / by Patricia Ryon Quiri.
     p.   cm. — (A First book)
   Includes bibliographical references and index.
   Summary: Describes the life and work of Alexander Graham Bell, from his invention of the telephone to the development of instruments to help the hearing impaired.
   ISBN 0-531-20022-1
   1. Bell, Alexander Graham, 1847–1922—Juvenile literature.
   2. Inventors—United States—Biography—Juvenile literature.
   [1. Bell, Alexander Graham, 1847–1922. 2. Inventors.] I. Title.
   II. Series.
JUV TK6143.B4Q57   1991
621.385'092—dc20
[B]   90-13095
                                       CIP
                                       AC

CONTENTS

ALEXANDER GRAHAM BELL

Telephones have become necessities in our world—we could hardly conduct our personal or business lives without them.

INTRODUCTION

The sound of the telephone and the telephone itself are familiar to just about everyone. These days most people have at least one telephone in their house or apartment. This instrument is used for many different reasons: calling a friend to chat, inviting someone to play, calling the doctor when someone is sick. In emergencies the telephone is a lifeline. You can reach the police or fire department in seconds.

The telephone is a means of communication. Communication is the way people exchange information. Perhaps your grandparents live in a different city or country than you. It's a treat to talk to them on the phone and tell them what you have been doing. This is communicating. The telephone is the instrument you use to communicate.

Using the phone to call a friend, a store, the doctor, your grandparents, your parents, or the police is a way of life today. Telephones are considered a necessity rather than a luxury. This was not the case, however, until well into the twentieth century. How different life must have been before the invention of the telephone! What in the world inspired Alexander Graham Bell to invent the telephone?

1 YOUNG ALEXANDER BELL

Alexander Bell was born in Edinburgh, Scotland, on March 3, 1847. He shared his birthday with his grandfather Bell. Alexander Bell also shared something else with his grandfather: they had the same name. In fact, young Alexander's father was also named Alexander. However, his father's full name was Alexander Melville Bell.

Young Alexander was not given a middle name at birth, so when he was eleven years old he did something about it. After meeting a family friend from Cuba whose name was Alexander Graham, he decided to take "Graham" as his middle name. He felt his new middle name would give him his own identity. Some people called him Graham; others called him Aleck.

11

As a young boy, Alexander Graham Bell was interested in lots of things. There was no limit to his curiosity. He had a remarkable gift for sounds and tones and played the piano very well. In fact, he took piano lessons from one of the most accomplished pianists of that time, Signor Auguste Benoit Bertini. His mother encouraged these lessons as she too was a good pianist. This was quite an accomplishment since Mrs. Bell was nearly deaf.

There was a special closeness between young Aleck and his mother. While others spoke to her through a rubber ear tube (a hearing device), Aleck did not. He found that by speaking in low tones close to her forehead, his mother could understand what he said. Taking the time and effort to do this was typical of Aleck's kind nature.

Scientific matters also interested Aleck. He and his older brother, Melville, collected plants and dead animals, including mice, toads, rabbits, dogs, and cats. They studied the animals' bodies by dissecting them (cutting them open).

Aleck was interested in speech sounds. This isn't surprising because both his father and grandfather were noteworthy speech teachers. Aleck was creative enough to experiment with sounds on his dog. By gently pressing on his dog's

This old photograph from the mid-nineteenth century shows (left to right) Aleck, Melville, and Edward Bell standing with their parents.

mouth and voice box, he could get noises out of the dog that sounded something like "How are you, Grandmama?" Imagine his family's surprise at a talking dog!

Young Aleck's grandfather, Alexander Bell, played a big part in shaping Aleck's interests. Grandfather Bell taught speech in London. He enjoyed the theater very much and would often read William Shakespeare's plays when teaching his students. He was a bit of an actor, a talent which seemed to be passed on to many of the Bells.

When Aleck was fifteen years old, he went to London to live for a year with his grandfather. He was going to continue his educational studies with Grandfather Bell. Under the elder man's tutelage, Aleck really buckled down. With his dramatic style, his grandfather made learning exciting. Aleck made good use of the house library. He especially enjoyed the books on speech, as well as the plays by Shakespeare. Grandfather Bell put the finishing touches on Aleck's own speech.

After spending the year with his grandfather, Aleck felt quite grown up for his age. He also had a new direction for his life. Instead of pursuing his earlier ambition to become a great musician,

Alexander Bell, Aleck's grandfather, was not only the namesake of Alexander Graham Bell, but a great influence on the boy as well.

Aleck now wanted to study sound and become a teacher of speech.

After his return from London, Aleck worked on another experiment involving sound. He and his brother Melville decided to make a "talking machine" with the parts that animals use to make sounds—mouth, tongue, throat, windpipe, and lungs.

Using their knowledge of how human speech sounds are made, they put together their machine. They made a head with a large mouth out of a tough plastic substance called gutta-percha. They made the throat out of tin and used a rubber tube for the windpipe. (They did not construct a tongue.) They placed a bellows in a box to act as lungs, and used it to blow air into the windpipe. They manipulated the windpipe and throat so that a sound would come through the mouth.

Their talking machine made a sound like the word "mama." The two teenagers had a great time playing tricks on their neighbors, who thought a real baby was crying!

Aleck Bell's interest in communication and inventing stayed with him his whole life. His father, Alexander Melville Bell, was a very successful speech teacher and elocutionist, and influenced this direction in Aleck's life. An elocutionist is someone who is a very good speaker and speaks in front of lots of people. Aleck's father often gave talks at the University of Edinburgh. In 1864 Alexander Melville Bell made up a system of written symbols called "visible speech." The symbols showed how the palate (roof of the mouth), tongue, and teeth should be positioned when saying a particular word. This could be done in English, Chinese, French, or any other language.

Some people didn't believe in Alexander Melville Bell's "visible speech." To prove it really did work, Mr. Bell had his two older sons, Melville and Aleck, perform. The boys left the room while the men thought up words. Mr. Bell then wrote down the symbols for these on a chalkboard. The boys came back into the room and correctly recognized the words. One man tried playing a trick on the boys. Instead of giving them a word to figure out, he made up a sound. Aleck and Melville studied the visible speech symbols and identified the right sound, which was something like a yawn. The men were amazed and quickly changed their minds about Alexander Melville Bell's "visible speech." This system was eventually used as an aid in teaching the deaf to speak.

Alexander Melville Bell, pictured above,
had to prove that his visible speech
system worked. It did, and later Aleck
would use it to help
deaf children learn to speak.

As a child and as an adult, Alexander Graham Bell was constantly inquisitive, yet never content to stick with one idea or experiment for a long stretch of time. With his brilliant mind and curious nature, he pursued the many different areas of research in the scientific world, even if it meant putting a previous experiment on hold. However, whatever he explored or studied at any particular time he did with total concentration. He enjoyed working late at night when all was quiet. Many times he would work on experiments until he was physically exhausted.

When Aleck was only sixteen, he taught music and speech at a boys' school in the city of Elgin, in northern Scotland, about 100 miles (160 km) away from his home. While he was there, Aleck experimented with tuning forks. A tuning fork is a metal instrument with two prongs. When it is struck, it vibrates and a tone is heard. He found that when one tuning fork vibrated, another fork that had the same tone would also vibrate. At the time of his own experiments, there was someone else working with tuning forks, the famous German scientist Hermann von Helmholtz. Apparently Helmholtz made some discoveries before Aleck, which of course was very disappointing for

Aleck. However, after these and his own discoveries, Aleck felt sure that someday speech would be sent over a wire. He did not know then that it would be his own voice that would clinch that place in history.

This photograph of Alexander Graham Bell, taken when he was about sixteen years old, is among a group of photos Bell selected for preservation.

2 TRAGEDY AND RECOVERY

Tragedy struck the Bell household in the late 1860s. Aleck's younger brother, Edward Charles, died of tuberculosis in 1867. Less than three years later his brother Melville also died of the same disease. Aleck, too, began to show signs of the dreaded sickness. He was exhausted from his teaching and from attending universities in Edinburgh and London.

In an effort to fight this illness, the Bells moved to Ontario, Canada. They felt the climate in Canada would be better for Aleck. It took the Bell family fourteen days to cross the Atlantic Ocean. Aleck was twenty-three years old.

Aleck's father bought a house just a few miles from a town called Brantford. Here Aleck's health

22

improved, and he grew stronger every day. He made friends with some of the Mohawk Indians in the area, who made him an honorary member of their tribe. The Mohawks taught Aleck how to do a war dance. He would often do his Indian dance when he became excited about something.

While he was recovering, Aleck kept working with tuning forks. He would also use the piano in his experiments. Often he would press one key at a time and sit there listening, totally absorbed in the tone. He was combining his knowledge of sound with his sensitive ear to figure out a way to improve the telegraph. At the time, the telegraph could send only one message over a wire. Aleck was trying to invent a telegraph that could send more than one message on the same wire. He called this a "multiple" (meaning more than one) or "harmonic" telegraph.

Alexander Graham Bell was twenty-four years old when he moved to Boston, Massachusetts. His health was good; the climate in Brantford had done wonders for him. Now he was making a new life for himself. He was in Boston to initiate the "visible speech" system. Aleck was going to teach deaf

In 1872 Bell opened a school of vocal
physiology and mechanics in Boston.
Here he teaches a deaf child to speak.

children, as well as other teachers of the deaf, the "visible speech" method.

Boston was a busy place. Colleges, universities, inventors, science, industry, and the seaport all were swarming around him. What better place for a young man with hopes of inventing? Aleck was very busy. He taught during the day. At night he continued his experiments with tuning forks, hoping to make a multiple telegraph.

It was in Boston that Alexander Graham Bell met a young man named Tom Watson. The twenty-year-old Watson worked in an electric shop owned by a Mr. Charles Williams, Jr. Watson worked with many different inventors and knew a great deal about electricity. When the two men met, Watson was surprised by Aleck's appearance. Aleck was a tall, thin man with a pale face, intense eyes, and a large nose. He had a moustache, black hair, and big black sideburns. He was dressed in good but worn clothes and was well-groomed. What impressed Watson most was how Bell spoke. His speech was beautiful—clear and concise.

Watson was fascinated with this man who was in every sense of the word a gentleman. He had seen all types of inventors before, and most could hardly be described as gentlemen.

Aleck, in turn, was impressed with Watson, whose knowledge of electricity and ability to construct models were awesome. Aleck had the knowledge to plan and draw models. His hands were clumsy, however, when it came to the actual construction. This was where he needed help. Watson readily agreed to help Aleck to build a model of the multiple telegraph. This was the beginning of their friendship and working relationship.

Little did Thomas A. Watson know when he met Bell that together they would forever change the business of communication.

3 HARD WORK

As usual, Alexander Graham Bell was very busy. He taught speech at Boston University during the day, worked on his experiments with Tom Watson at night, and in between tutored deaf children. One of those children was young George Sanders. His father, Thomas Sanders, was a wealthy man who took an interest in Aleck's multiple telegraph. He agreed to supply Aleck with the money needed to work on his experiments.

Another private pupil was Mabel Hubbard, a sixteen-year-old girl with whom Aleck eventually fell in love. Her deafness had been brought on by an attack of scarlet fever, and at age five she had been plunged into a world of silence. Mabel's father, Gardiner Greene Hubbard, enlisted Aleck's

*Thomas Sanders was the first to back
Bell's ideas financially.*

help in perfecting Mabel's speech. Mr. Hubbard had also taken an interest in young Mr. Bell's experiments. He, too, agreed to support Aleck's work on the multiple telegraph. Mr. Sanders and Mr. Hubbard were Aleck's financial backers. They would give Aleck money to work on his experiments, and in return they would get a share of the eventual profits.

Aleck and Tom Watson worked endlessly during the evenings. They used the attic of Charles Williams's electric shop as a workshop for a while. It was hot up there, but they were so involved in their experiments that at times they didn't notice the heat. They worked with tuning forks, wires, batteries, and electromagnets. Aleck's sharp, sensitive ear would help in adjusting the sounds of the tuning forks. Experimenting and inventing is frustrating work. In those days, many people were trying to build a multiple telegraph, so it was a race to see who could perfect it and get a pat-

Gardiner Green Hubbard would eventually become Bell's father-in-law, but before that Hubbard was a financial supporter of Bell's work.

ent first. A patent is something an inventor has to apply for. Once it is granted, it gives the inventor the sole right for a certain number of years to make, use, or sell the invention. During Aleck's time, inventors had to go to Washington, D.C., to apply for their patents.

One night in the spring of 1875, frustration nagged at Aleck. The sounds sent across the wire could not be separated. They were always bunched up. Aleck was tired, hot, and disheartened. He knew he and Tom Watson were on the right track. Making the instrument work, however, was another story. It was then that Aleck told Tom about his ideas for a telephone.

During the previous summer, the summer of 1874, back home near Brantford, Ontario, Aleck had figured out what was involved in making speech go across a wire. He had the basic idea of how to build a telephone. The word "telephone" comes from two Greek words: *tele*, meaning far off and *phone*, meaning sound. Seemingly, the people skilled in the electrical field had dedicated themselves only to the telegraph. Perhaps they never dreamed of a different way of communicating as Aleck did.

Aleck and Tom Watson thought they could turn Aleck's idea into a device that would carry words over a wire. The two men were very excited about this. But when Aleck spoke to his two financial backers, Mr. Sanders and Mr. Hubbard, neither man thought the telephone would be of any use. They angrily urged him to concentrate on the multiple telegraph.

But Aleck did receive some encouragement for his idea from an important person. He was Joseph Henry, one of the world's leading physicists and director of the Smithsonian Institution in Washington, D.C. While Aleck was securing his patent for the not yet perfected multiple telegraph, he made an appointment to see Dr. Henry. The older man was impressed with the model of the multiple telegraph.

Aleck also told Dr. Henry about his ideas for the telephone, and Dr. Henry listened carefully. Aleck told him he had a problem: he did not have much knowledge of electricity. He thought perhaps he should publish his idea and let someone else make the telephone. Dr. Henry gave Aleck some simple and direct advice. He told him he must pursue this invention himself, and if he didn't have the electrical knowledge, he must somehow *"Get it!"*

4 THE PAYOFF

After a while Aleck took time off from his teaching to devote all his time to his experiments. He didn't have much money to live on. His meals were limited, and he didn't sleep enough. Time was important. He and Tom Watson continued their work on the multiple telegraph. What endless energy they had! Most nights ended in disappointment, but on June 2, 1875, fate seemed to be on their side.

At this time they were working with organ reeds in place of the tuning forks. The sounds from the reeds vibrated longer and could be tuned better. Watson, in one room, would make the reed on the transmitter vibrate. Bell, in another room, would receive the sounds of the vibrations.

This view of Alexander Graham Bell's workshop
is now on display in the Boston
headquarters of the New England Telephone
and Telegraph Company.

Bell and Watson work on their
latest advancement.

On this particular day, one of the organ reeds on Watson's end got stuck. He had adjusted a screw too tightly. Meanwhile Bell, impatiently waiting for sounds, heard nothing. Watson tried to get the reed working again by flicking it with his finger. The sound of his finger striking the stuck reed was heard by Bell. It was a sound that was very different from the others. The sound rose and fell and varied in strength. It was a sound that probably no other person than Aleck could have determined to be different. However, Aleck's sensitive, musically trained ear knew it was different.

That small sound was a breakthrough. Aleck raced into the room where Watson was. The two men were elated! Because that sound had come across the wire, they knew it would be possible to get speech, which also varied in pitch and strength, over a wire. The invention of the telephone was now on its way!

Bell and Watson kept experimenting that night. They used different objects to strike the organ reed. Bell listened carefully with his super sense of hearing. Before they left the shop that night, Aleck drew a sketch of a telephone. Watson had it made the next day.

It took a lot of time, patience, and hard work on the part of both men. They made changes and

This painting shows Bell explaining something
to Watson in their living and working
quarters at 5 Exeter Place, Boston.

adjustments in their telephone. Words were heard over the wire but they could not be understood. Endless experimenting. Their invention was close to perfection when Bell felt the need for more privacy. He no longer wanted to use the attic in Williams's electric shop. Aleck decided to rent two rooms at 5 Exeter Place, which he and Watson used for both experimenting and sleeping. They devoted all their time to work on the telephone. Perfecting the multiple telegraph would have to wait.

Bell and Watson worked nonstop throughout the hot summer. Then Aleck became very sick. After a while he traveled back to his parents' house in Canada. He needed a lot of peace, quiet, and rest. While in Canada, he wrote out the detailed plans for the telephone, which were needed to get a patent, and sent them to a lawyer in Washington, D.C.

In the meantime, Aleck was waiting to hear about a patent application he had filed in England. He wanted to wait until that one was granted before filing the one in Washington. However, Gardiner Greene Hubbard, who now was interested in the telephone, became impatient and told the Washington lawyer to go ahead and apply for Bell's patent. This was done on February 14,

1876. It was a good thing he did because hours later on that very same day, a man named Elisha Gray went into the Patent Office with his own plans for a telephone. Imagine how different the history books would have been had Elisha Gray been first!

On March 7, 1876, Aleck received the patent for the telephone. He had returned from Canada, and he and Tom Watson were back to work at 5 Exeter Place. They were very busy making more changes on the telephone. The sounds that came across the wire were still unclear, so they built another transmitter. The wire that was connected to the diaphragm was put into a metal cup which contained diluted sulfuric acid. The diaphragm vibrated from sounds. When the diaphragm vibrated, the wire would go up or down in the acid as its resistance changed. This made the electric movement (or current) in the wire leading to the receiver undulate (or rise and fall). The end result at the receiver would be sound. This sounds pretty complicated, but the two men thought it would work.

It was now March 10. Watson got the instrument ready for testing. He was in one room; Bell was in the other. Watson lifted the receiver and placed it on his ear. Moments later, the first telephone message in history was sent and received.

*Through this historic instrument the first
telephone conversation was held!*

Bell's voice came over the wire loud and clear.
"Mr. Watson, come here. I want you!"

Watson dashed into the room to see Bell. Sulfuric acid had spilled onto Bell's clothes. Their ex-

Watson rushes in to Bell after hearing the first telephone message: "Watson, come here. I want you."

*How things have changed:
switchboards were needed
for every call in 1882 (left).
Today, only some international
calls need an operator's help.*

citement was so great they forgot the acid. They kept talking to each other over the telephone that night. Bell, only twenty-nine years old, realized this was an invention that would profoundly change the world.

5 CONTINUED SUCCESS

The United States of America was celebrating its one hundredth birthday, called the Centennial Celebration, in 1876. A big exposition was being held in Philadelphia. On exhibit were all sorts of things related to art, science, history, and the latest technological developments. The great inventions of the past year were also to be on display. Mabel Hubbard, who was now engaged to Aleck Bell, urged her fiancé to show his telephone. He arrived at the exposition on Saturday, June 24, and went about setting up his instruments. Since Tom Watson could not be with him, Mabel's cousin Willie Hubbard was to join Aleck later that night.

The next day was a typically hot summer day

in Philadelphia. Because it was Sunday the exhibits were closed to all except the judges. The day dragged. Everyone was hot and tired. Aleck was afraid his display would not be looked at. This was disappointing because he had to be back in Boston the next day. Just as the judges were about to leave, the exposition's guest of honor recognized Aleck. The guest of honor was Dom Pedro, emperor of Brazil. In his party were many scientists, including Sir William Thomson, who was one of the most famous scientists in the world.

Dom Pedro knew Aleck from Boston. He had been very interested in Aleck's method for teaching deaf students. When he saw Aleck in the Exposition Hall, he turned to his tired group and insisted they have a look at Aleck's invention.

Aleck went across the hall to where the transmitter was hooked up. The men in Dom Pedro's party took turns with the receiver. Incredibly they heard a voice—Alexander Graham Bell's clear, distinct, beautiful voice. Aleck recited a quotation from Shakespeare's *Hamlet* which begins "To be, or not to be, that is the question . . ." Dom Pedro is said to have exclaimed "My God! It speaks!" as well as "I hear! I hear!" Amazement buzzed throughout the group. It seemed incredible to hear

Telegraphic and
Telephonic
Apparatus
By A Graham Bell.

*At the Centennial Exposition in Philadelphia,
Alexander Graham Bell publicly
demonstrated the telephone.*

a voice from across the room sound as though it had been right next to them! The instrument never worked better. Sir William Thomson hailed it as the most wonderful invention he had seen in America. Alexander Graham Bell received an award from the judges at the exposition for his invention of the telephone.

In July of 1877, Aleck Bell and Mabel Hubbard were married. The ceremony took place at the Hubbard home on Brattle Street in Boston. Before the wedding, Aleck gave Mabel two gifts. One was a pretty cross of pearls and the other was almost his very life. He had had a legal paper drawn up which gave Mabel all his rights in the new telephone company. The money made from his invention would go to Mabel. He also gave her all but ten of his shares of stock in the company. This was just one more way to show his love for her.

The happy couple honeymooned in Scotland and England. While in England, Aleck received an invitation to demonstrate the telephone to Queen Victoria. Assembled at the royal palace were the queen, her daughter Princess Beatrice, her son the duke of Connaught, and members of the royal party. Aleck explained the concept of

*Here Bell demonstrates the telephone
in Salem, Massachusetts.*

the telephone in terms he hoped would be understood. Then he gave a demonstration. He explained that the receiver was hooked up to Osborne Cottage, where Miss Kate Field, an American writer hired to help publicize the telephone, would sing into the transmitter.

Queen Victoria took the receiver and Aleck turned on the current. When Aleck looked back at the queen, he saw that she was talking to Princess Beatrice. To the astonishment of all in the room, he leaned down and touched Queen Victoria's hand. (The British have strict rules when it comes to addressing royalty. One does not touch the queen.) Aleck then told the queen to put the receiver to her ear and listen. She was so impressed with the telephone that she didn't seem to mind Aleck's breach of royal etiquette. In fact she even wanted to buy the two telephones used in the royal demonstration.

On January 25, 1915, the first coast-to-coast, or transcontinental, phone call was placed. This was nearly thirty-nine years after the first historic telephone call between Bell and Watson. Telephone lines now covered the countryside. Alexander Graham Bell, handsome and impressive with his gray hair, gray beard, and more portly

Mabel and Alexander Bell,
later in life

figure, was seated at a desk in New York with a telephone in front of him. Three thousand miles (4,800 km) away in California, Thomas A. Watson also sat beside a telephone. The instruments were readied. Would Bell's voice carry over the thousands of miles between the East Coast and the West Coast? It rang out loud and clear as Watson heard the familiar words "Mr. Watson, come here. I want you!" The first transcontinental phone call was a success! Alexander Graham Bell was sixty-seven years old.

Alexander Graham Bell was a very busy man throughout his life. Among his other achievements were the inventions of a photophone, which transmitted speech without wires; a device that aided the lungs of respiratory patients called a "vacuum jacket"; and a metal detector. He improved upon the phonograph and the hydrofoil speedboat. He studied flying and organized a group called the Aerial Experiment Association. Bell was also president of the National Geographic Society.

Throughout his life Alexander Graham Bell remained dedicated to his work with the deaf. He helped in the invention of an instrument called an audiometer, which measures deafness. A good

*Above: Bell helped direct the education of
Helen Keller, enabling her to learn to
communicate with the rest of the world.
Here, Helen Keller, left, talks to Bell and
her teacher, Annie Sullivan.
Left: on January 25, 1915, the New York-San
Francisco telephone line opened. Bell, in
New York (center of top picture), phoned Watson
in San Francisco (seated third from left in
bottom photo) with the same message used
thirty-nine years before.*

friend of Bell's, the famous Helen Keller, who was both deaf and blind, dedicated her autobiography to him. She wrote "To Alexander Graham Bell who has taught the deaf to speak . . ." Among all his accomplishments, teaching the deaf to speak was perhaps the most joyous.

ACTIVITIES

"Tuning" Forks

Materials needed
table forks of different sizes and types

Steps
1. Take one fork and tap it on a table.
2. Quickly put the fork to your ear.
3. Listen to the sound.
4. Repeat steps 1–3 with the other forks.
5. Observe the different pitches.

Alexander Graham Bell did a lot of work with tuning forks. By doing the above experiment, you can get an idea of how tuning forks work. The mass (weight) of the fork's tines determines the pitch you hear.

Make Your Own "Telephone"

Materials needed
2 paper cups, 2 paper clips, scissors, string, 2 people

Steps
1. Poke a hole in the bottoms of the two cups.
2. Cut a piece of string about 25 feet (7.5 m) long.
3. Pull one end of the string through the bottom of one cup.
4. Fasten a paper clip to the string inside the cup. Tie a knot. This will keep the string in place.
5. Repeat steps 3 and 4 with the other paper cup and the other end of the string.
6. Each person holds a cup. Walk away from each other so the string is taut.
7. One person holds cup to his or her ear while the other person talks into cup at the opposite end of the string.
8. Observe the sound that is transmitted from one cup to the other.

What happens
When one person speaks into the cup, the bottom of that cup vibrates. The bottom of the

cup is like a diaphragm. These vibrations travel along the string and through the bottom of the other cup. The bottom of this cup is also like a diaphragm. The sound waves are then heard by the listener. The result is sound.

Variations
Substitute plastic cups, tin cans, or oatmeal boxes for the paper cups. Substitute wire, ribbon, or rope for the string. Record your observations. Which materials transmit the best sounds?

FOR FURTHER READING

Boettinger, H. M. *The Telephone Book*. Croton-on-Hudson, N.Y.: Riverwood Publishers, 1977.

Costain, Thomas B. *The Chord of Steel*. Garden City, N.Y.: Doubleday, 1960.

Farr, Naunerle C. *Thomas Edison—Alexander Graham Bell*. West Haven, Conn.: Pendulum Press, 1979.

Johnson, Ann D. *The Value of Discipline: The Story of Alexander Graham Bell*. San Diego, Calif.: Oak Tree Publications, 1985.

Quackenbush, Robert. *Ahoy! Ahoy! Are You There?* Englewood Cliffs, N.J.: Prentice-Hall, 1981.

Shippen, Katherine B. *Mr. Bell Invents the Telephone*. New York: Random House, 1963.

INDEX

ABOUT THE AUTHOR

Patricia Ryon Quiri lives in Palm Harbor, Florida, with her husband and three sons. She is a former elementary school teacher and has an elementary education degree from Alfred University in New York State. Ms. Quiri is the author of the Franklin Watts book entitled *Dating*.